The Ray's Creations Coloring Book

"The Mandalas"

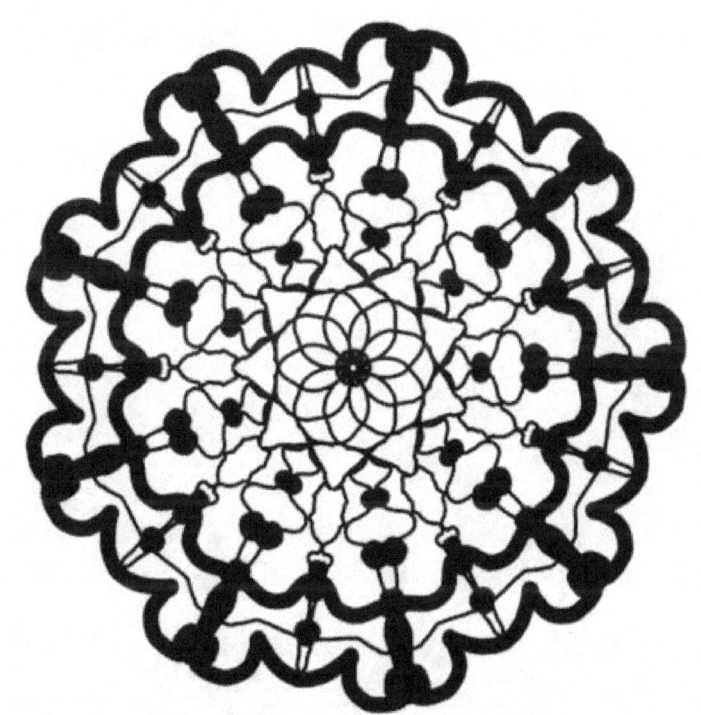

By Ray Tucker of Ray's Creations
raytuckerartist@gmail.com

This book is dedicated to my family, the thousands of students that I have shared my knowledge with, and my artist friends who have encouraged me in my creative art journey.

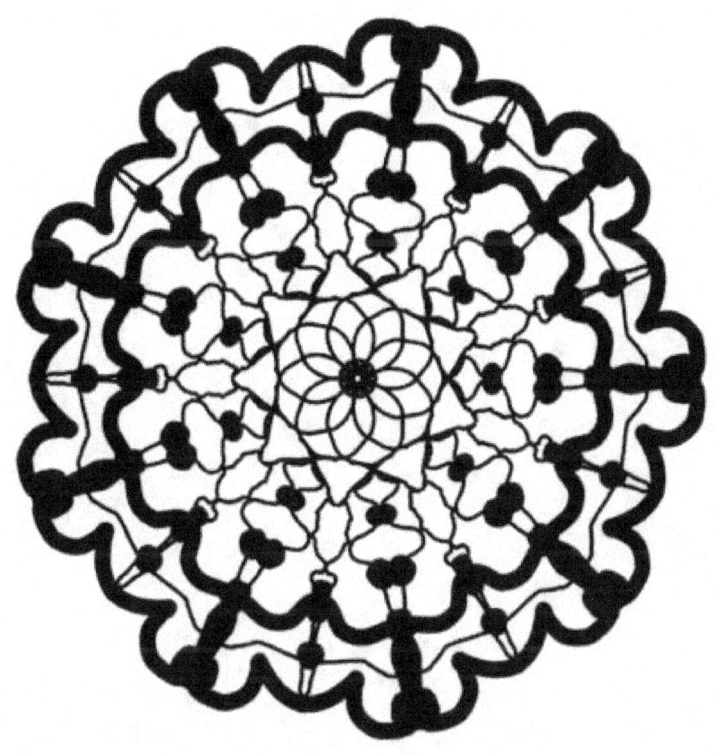

What is a Mandala?

Mandalas have existed since the beginning of time. Simply stated, a mandala is a sacred circle. The word mandala comes from the ancient Sanskrit language and loosely means "circle" or "center". It's a simple geometric shape that has no beginning or end. Within its circular shape, the mandala has the power to promote relaxation, balance the body's energies, enhance your creativity, and support healing. The great news is you can achieve all of these benefits while having fun with your mandala coloring pages.

So, take out your favorite color pencils (they work the best) or, color markers (they tend to bleed through the paper and are not the best choice) and have fun choosing your colors and filling in the spaces of each Mandala.

Note: For the best coloring results, use a
quality brand of color pencils. I prefer the
Prisma brand. Prisma color is highly pigmented.
The resulting image is vibrant and rich.
However, no matter what pencil brand you use, the benefits of
coloring are still the same. It helps to reduce stress,
can lower your blood pressure, and improve your creativity.

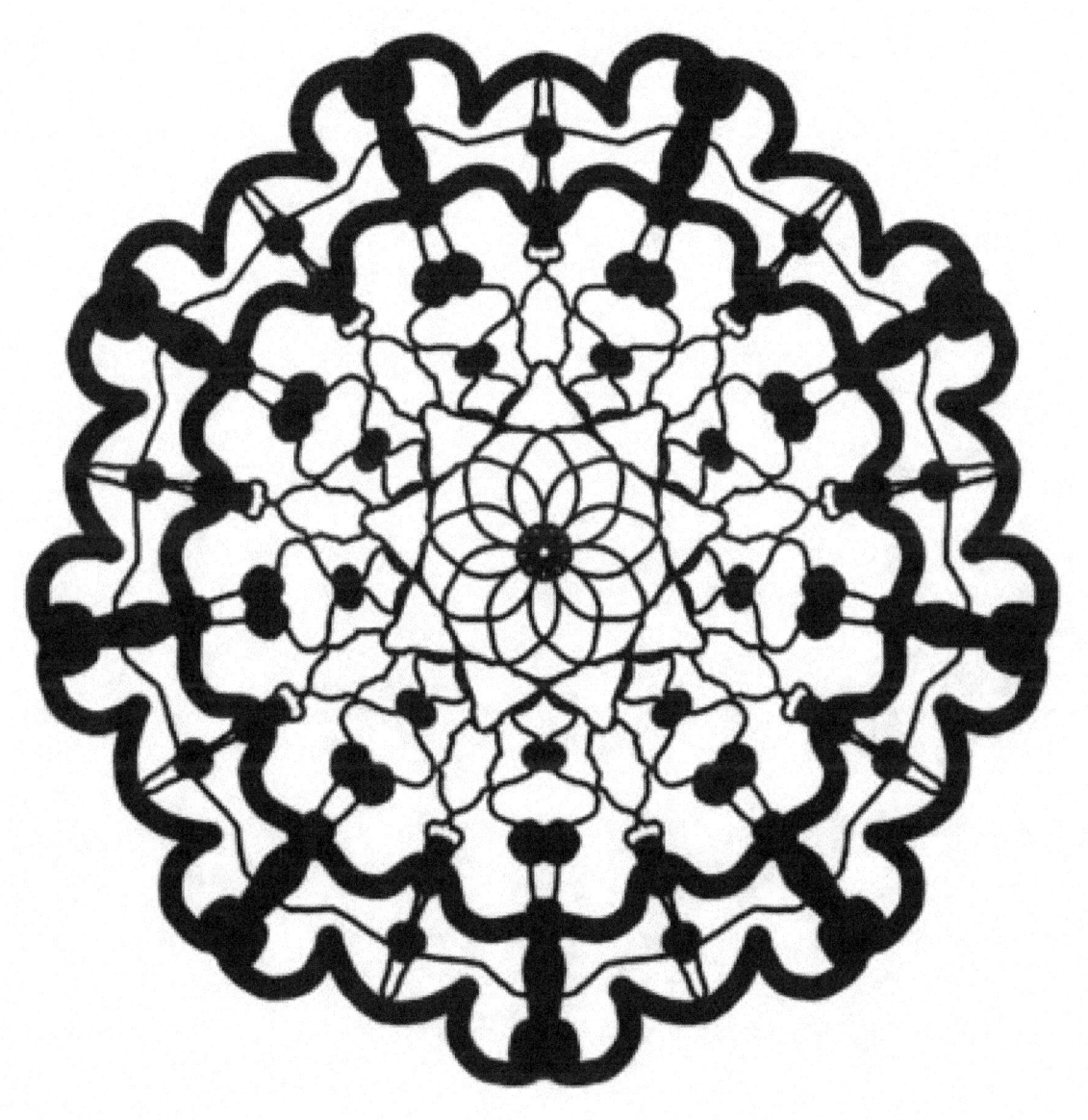

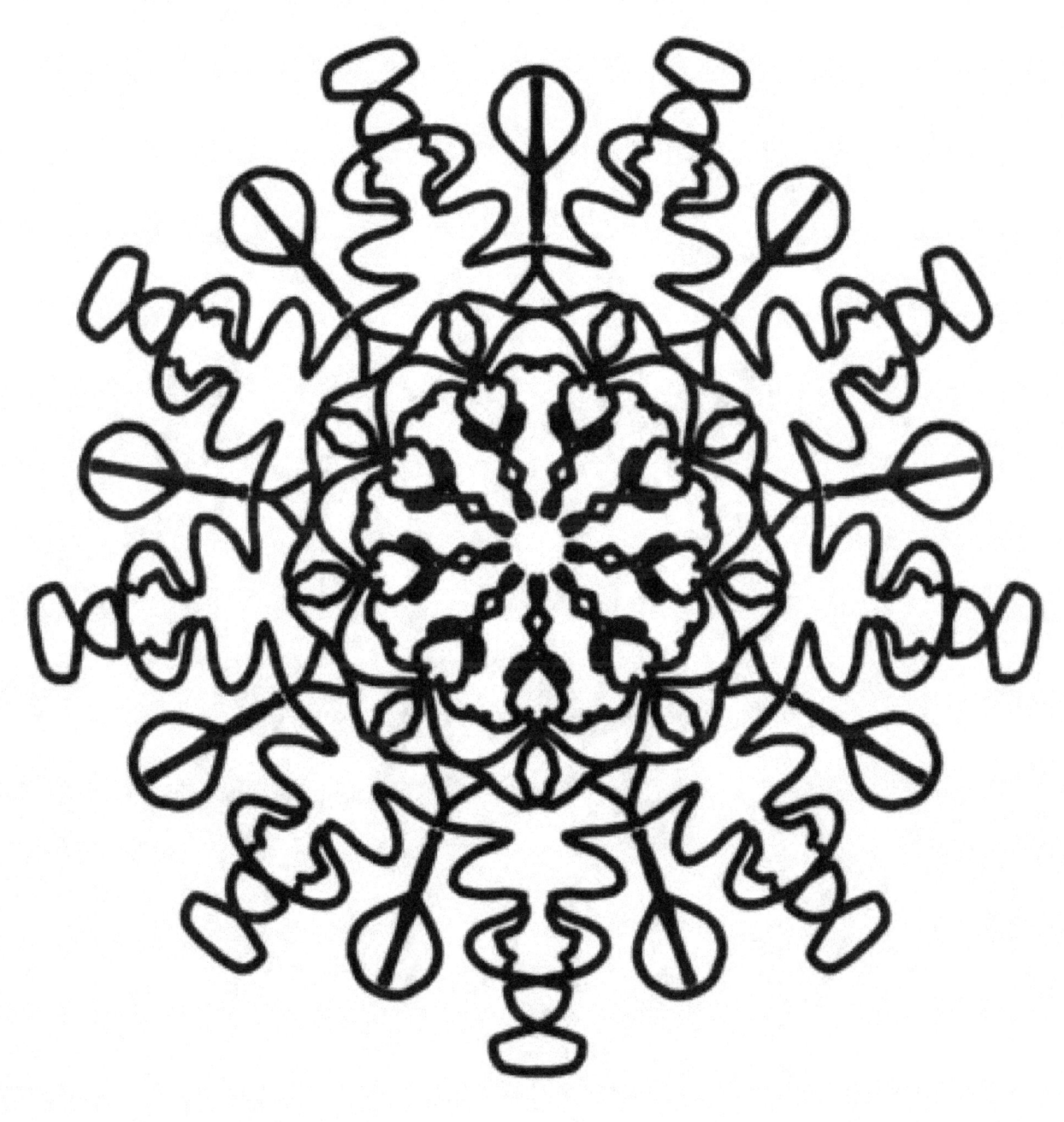

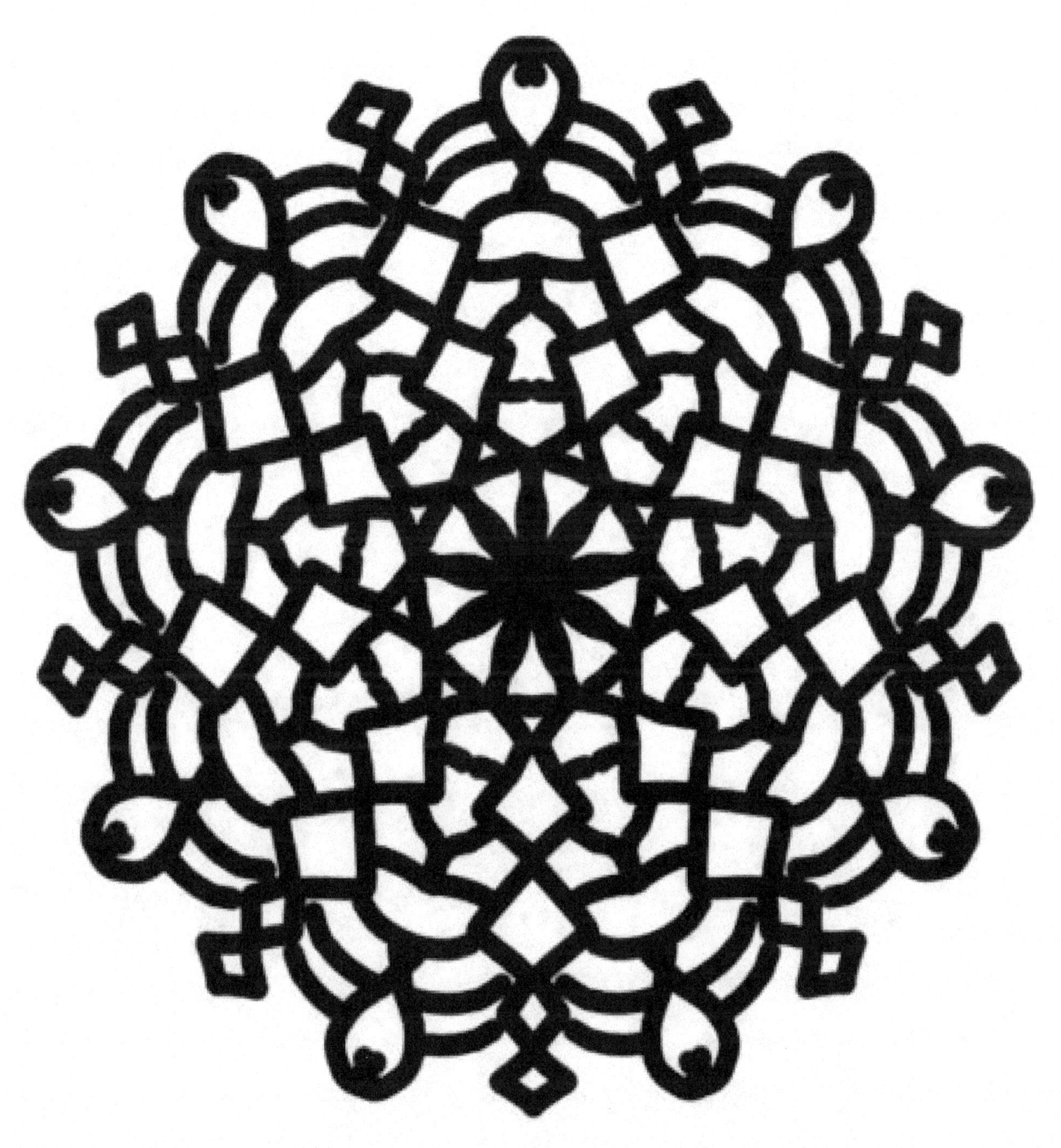

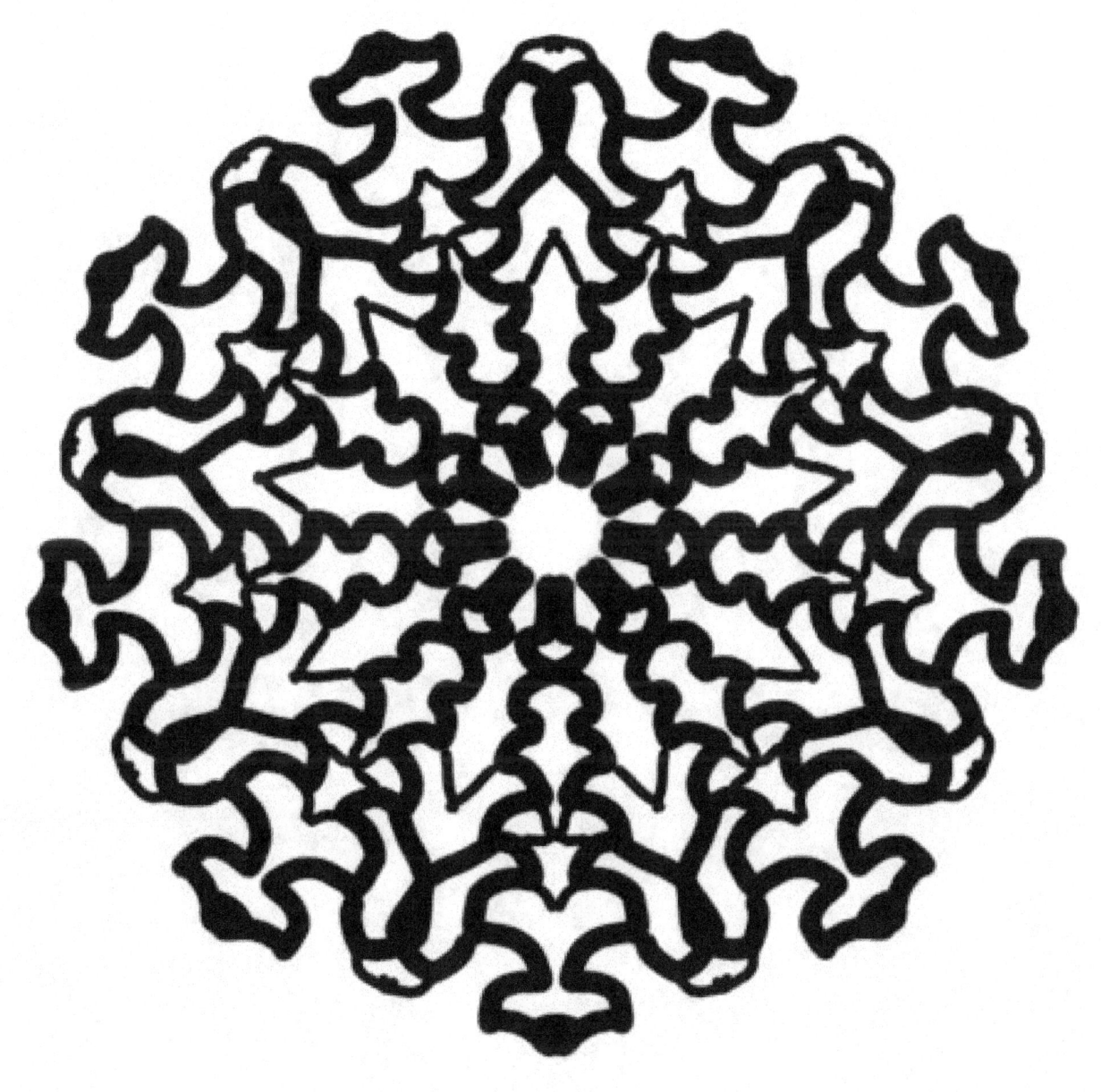

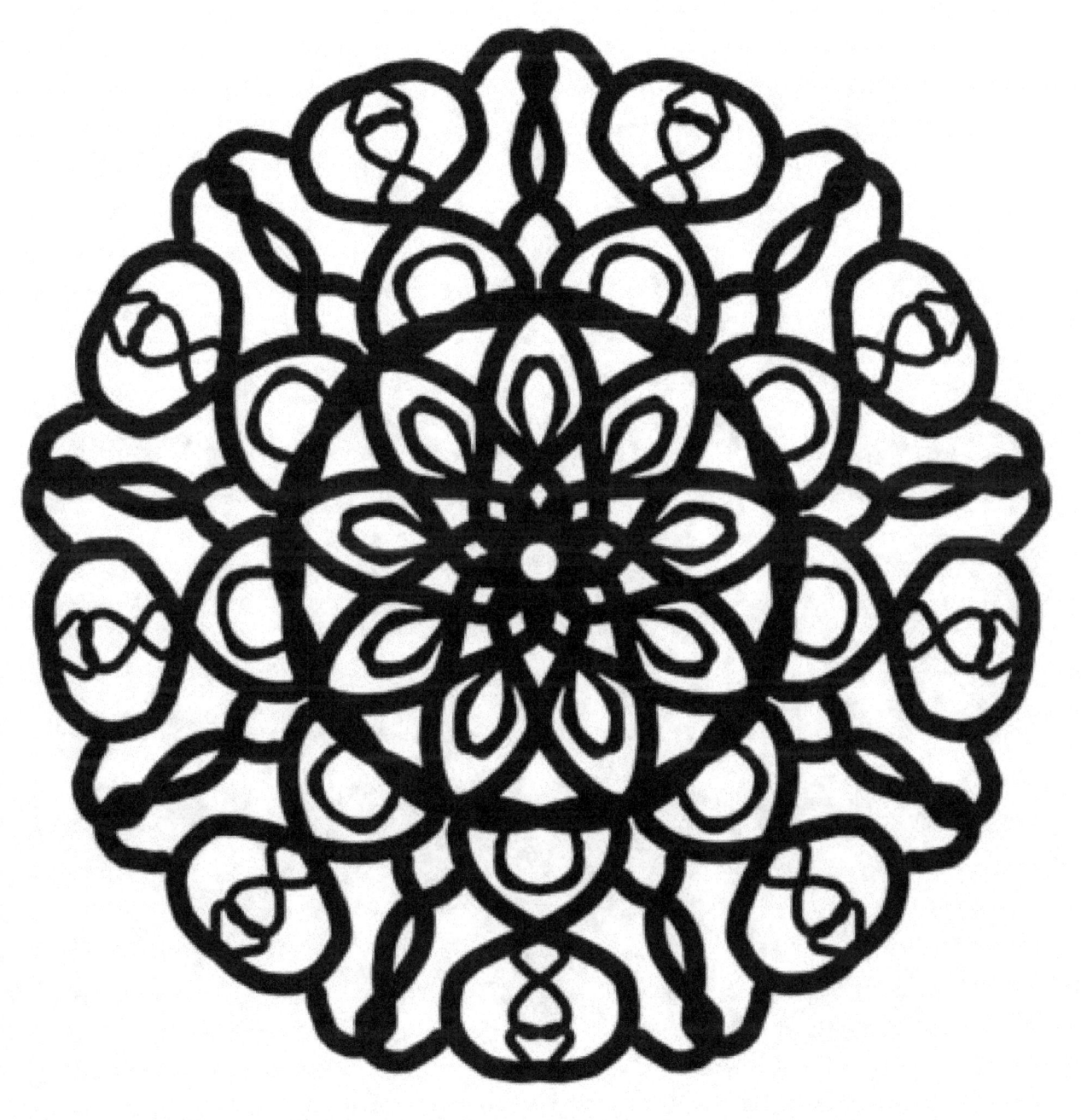

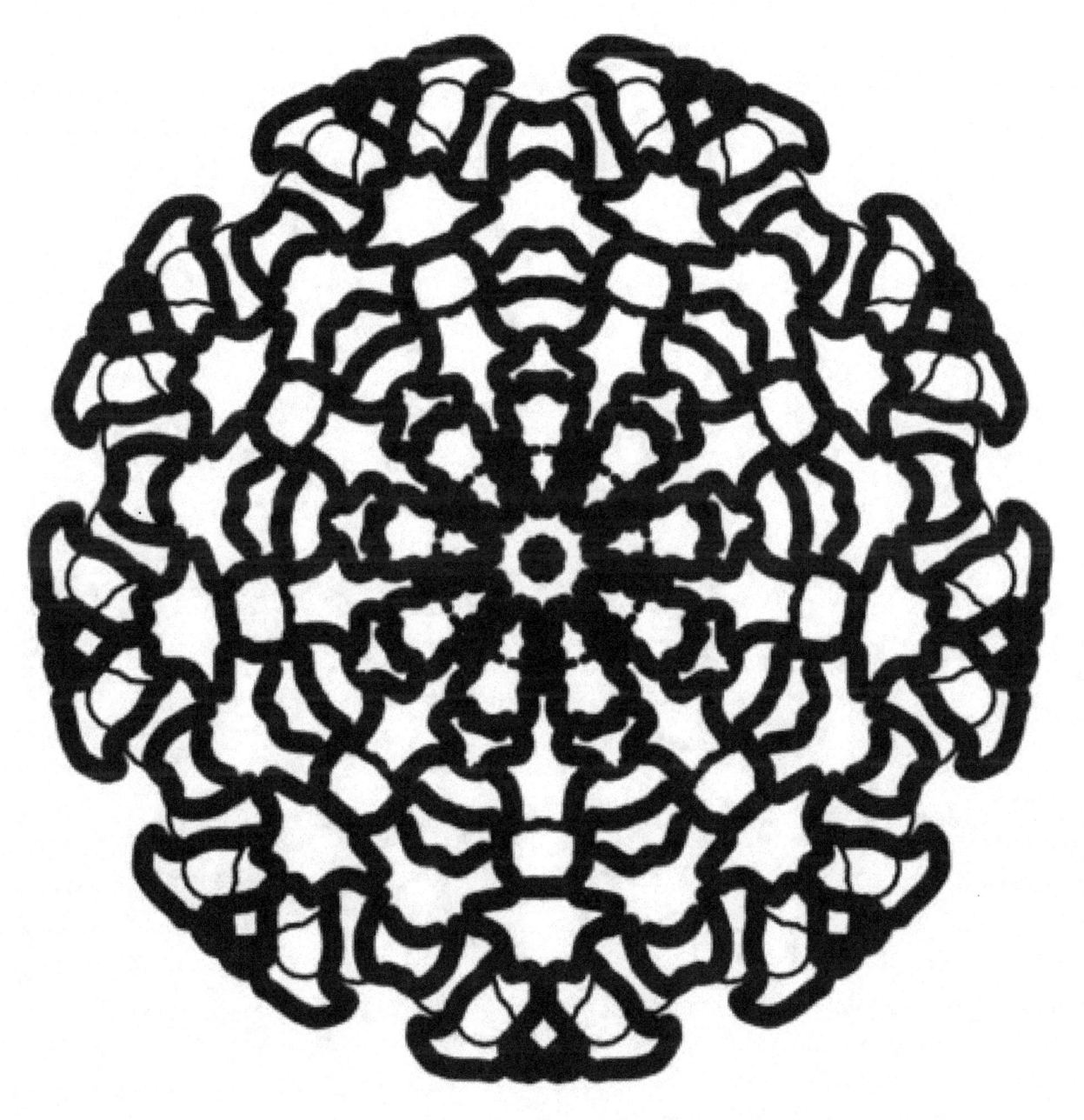

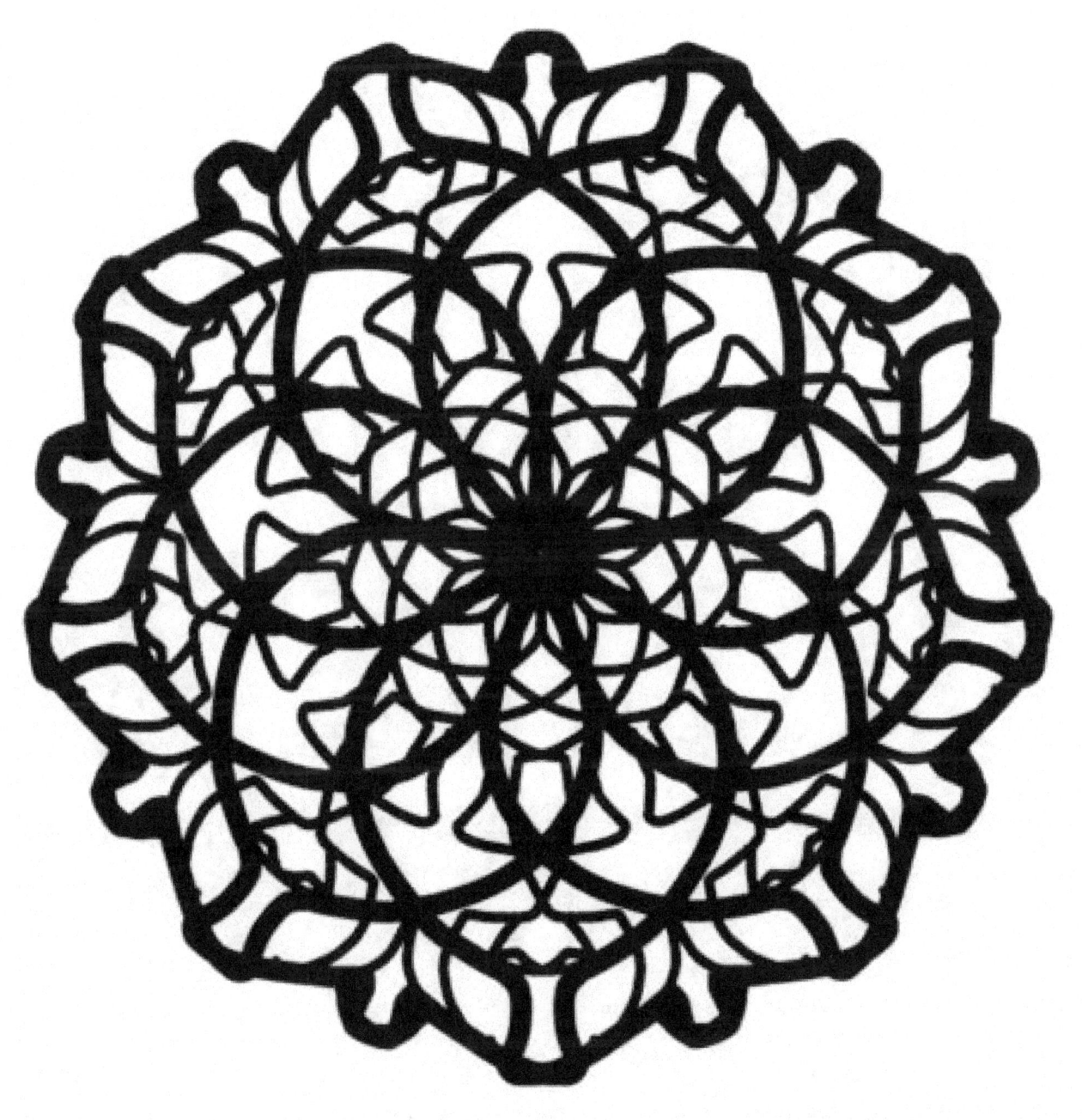

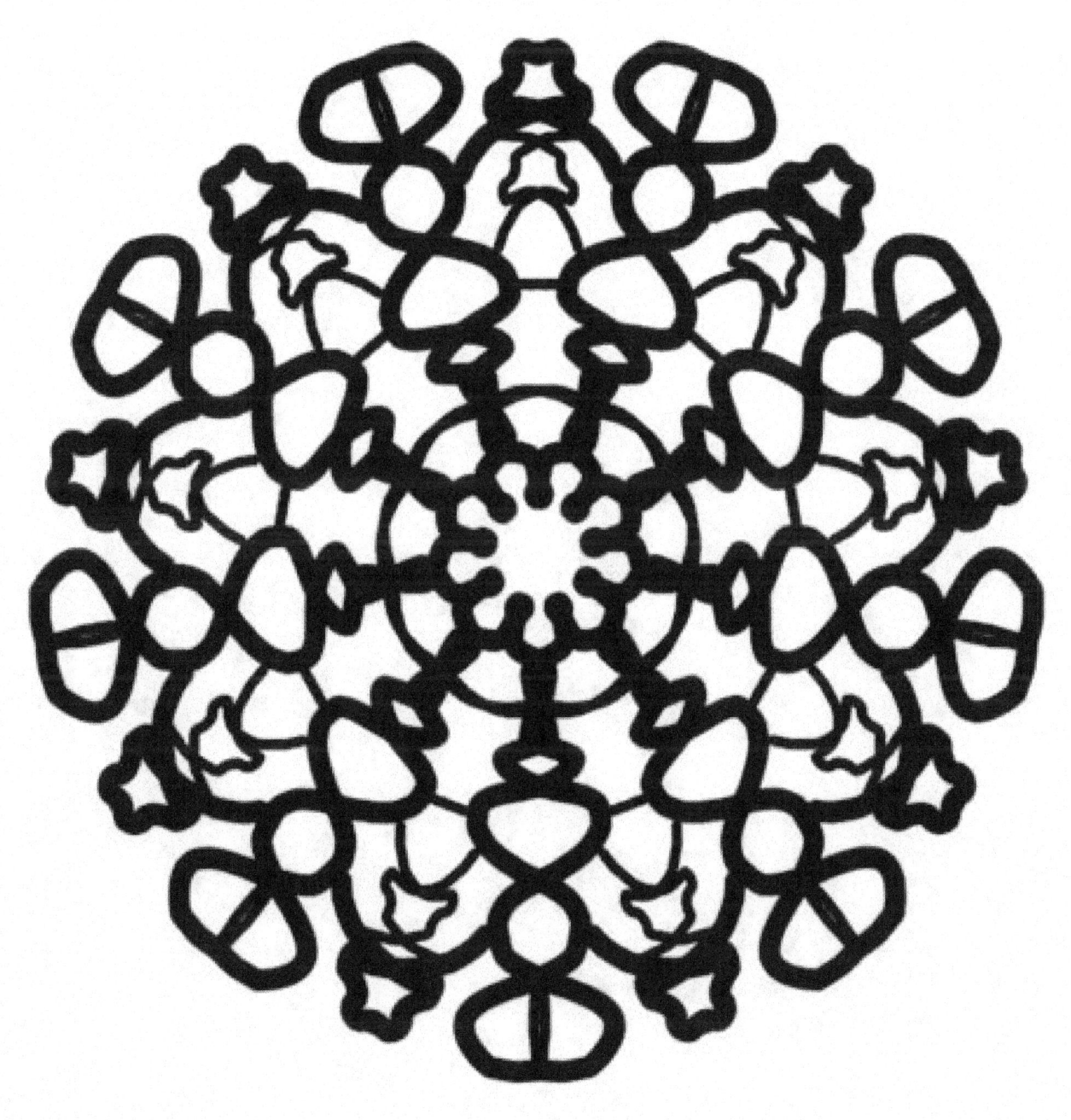

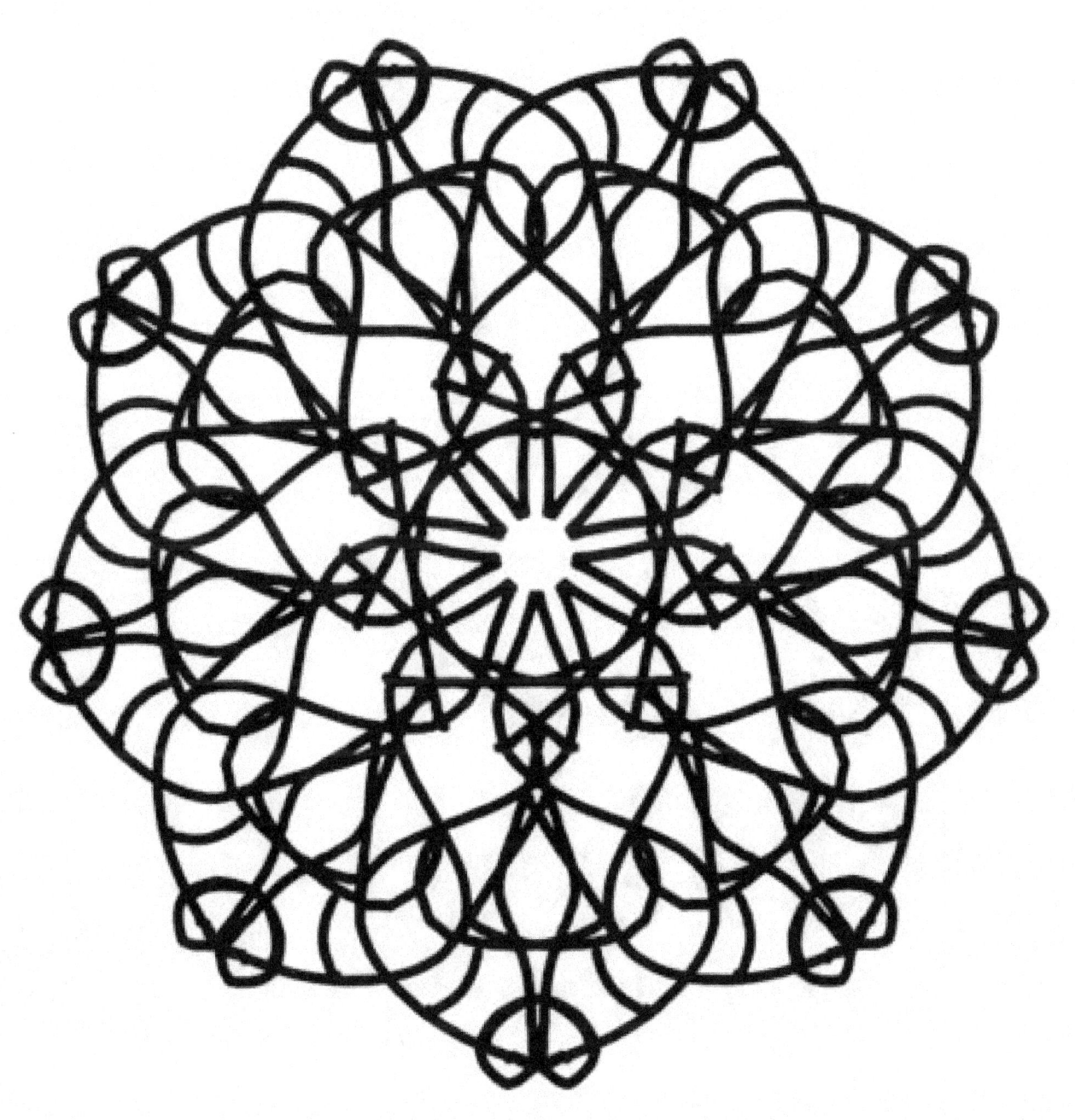

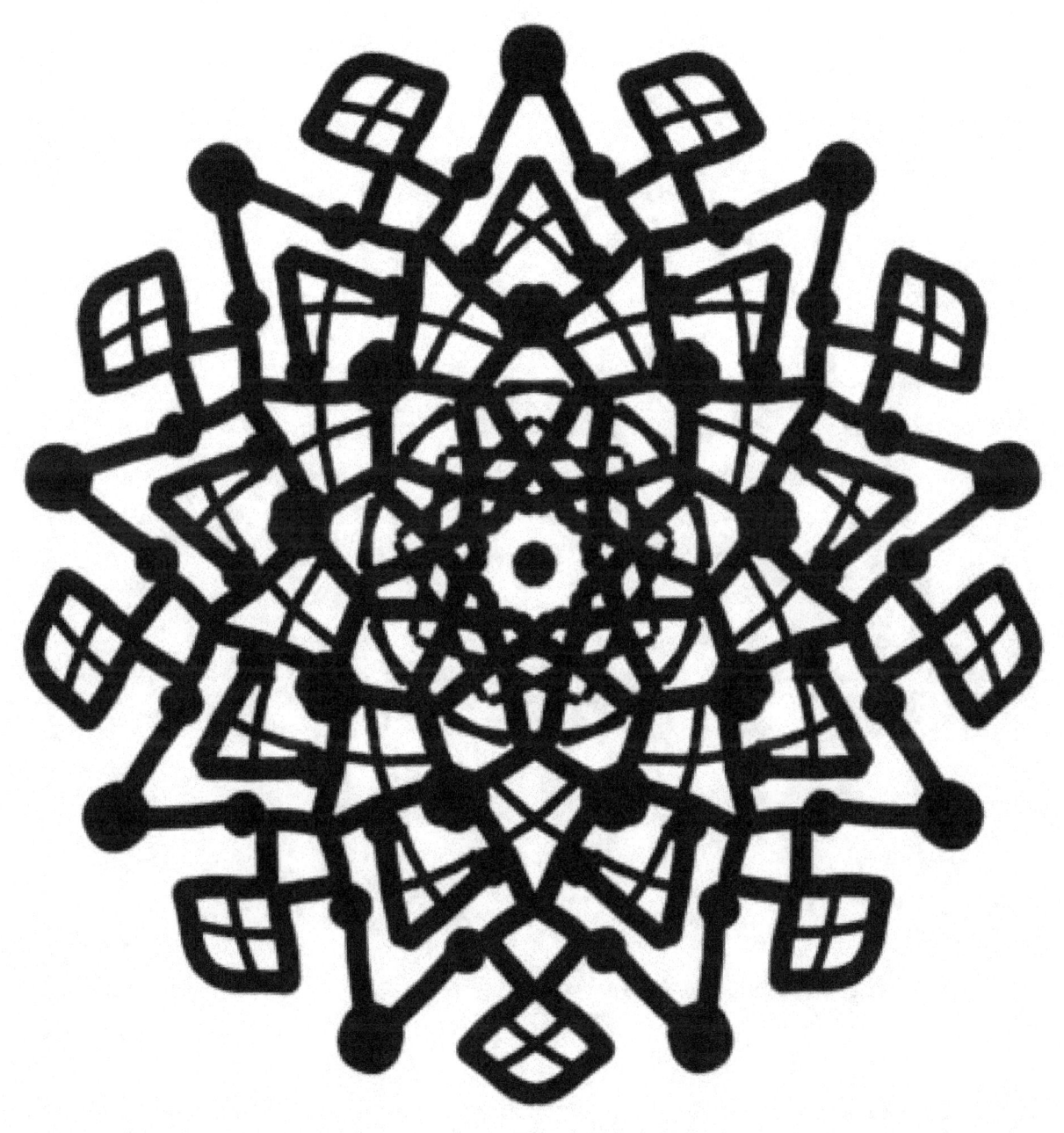

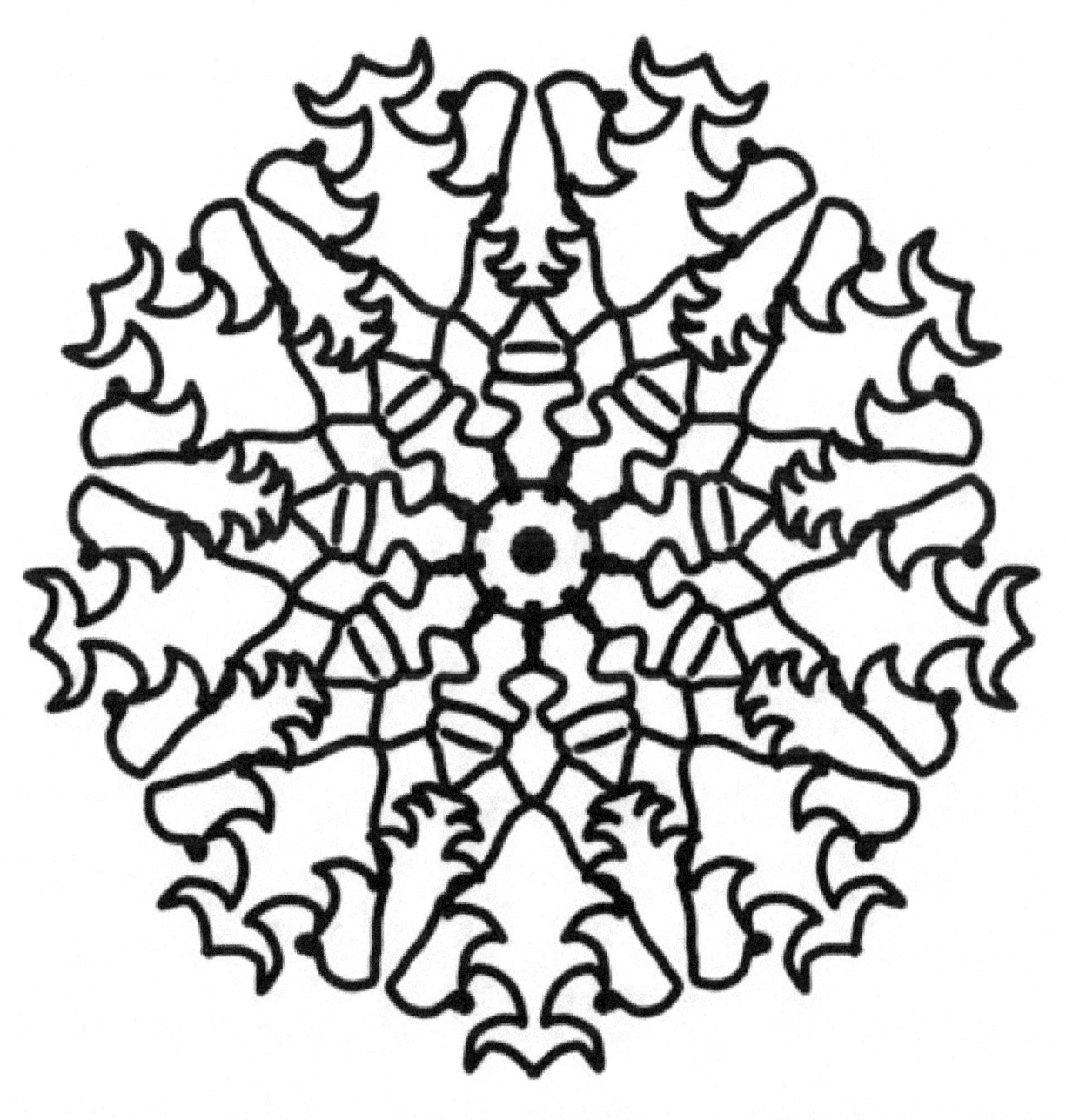

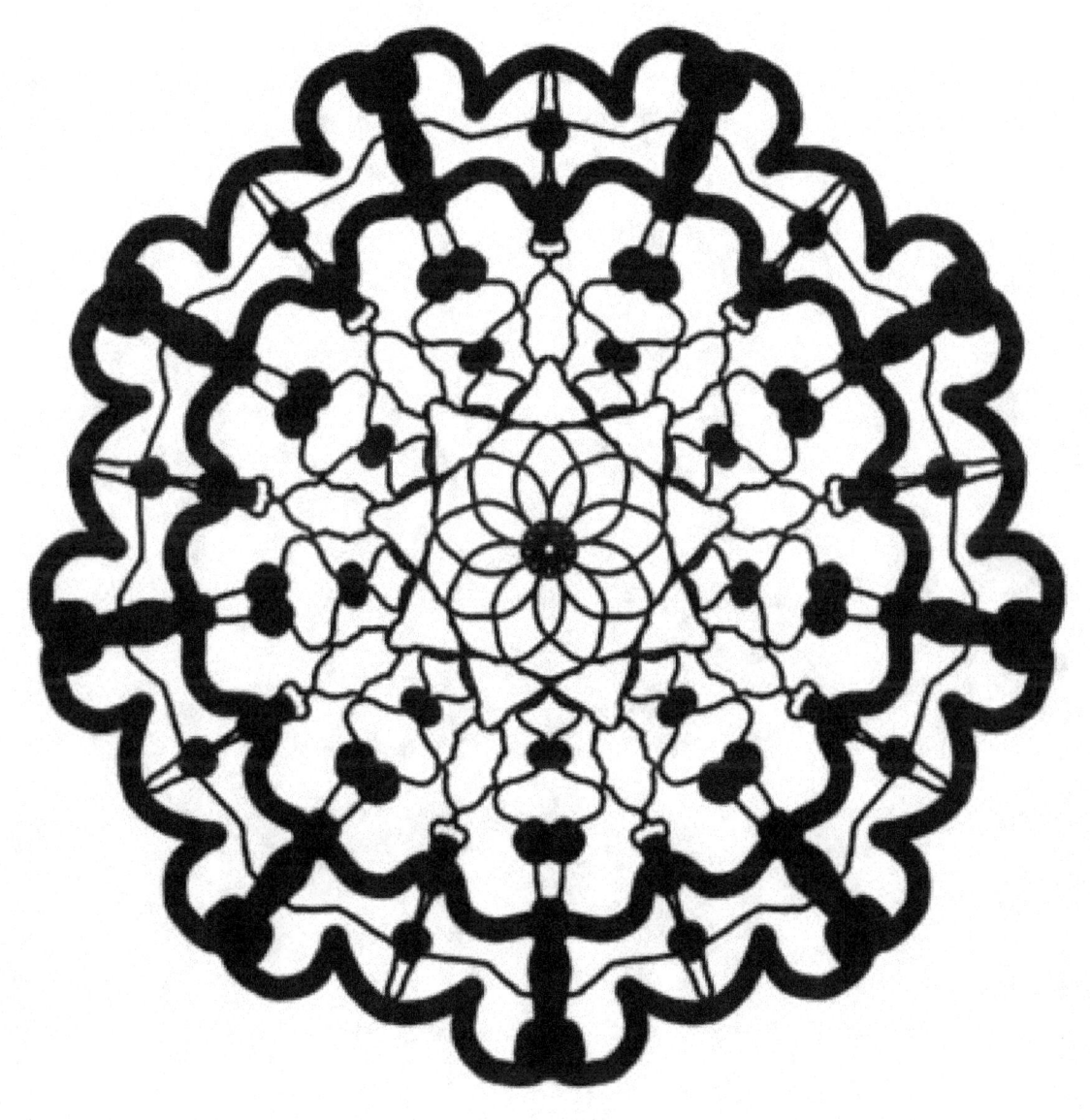

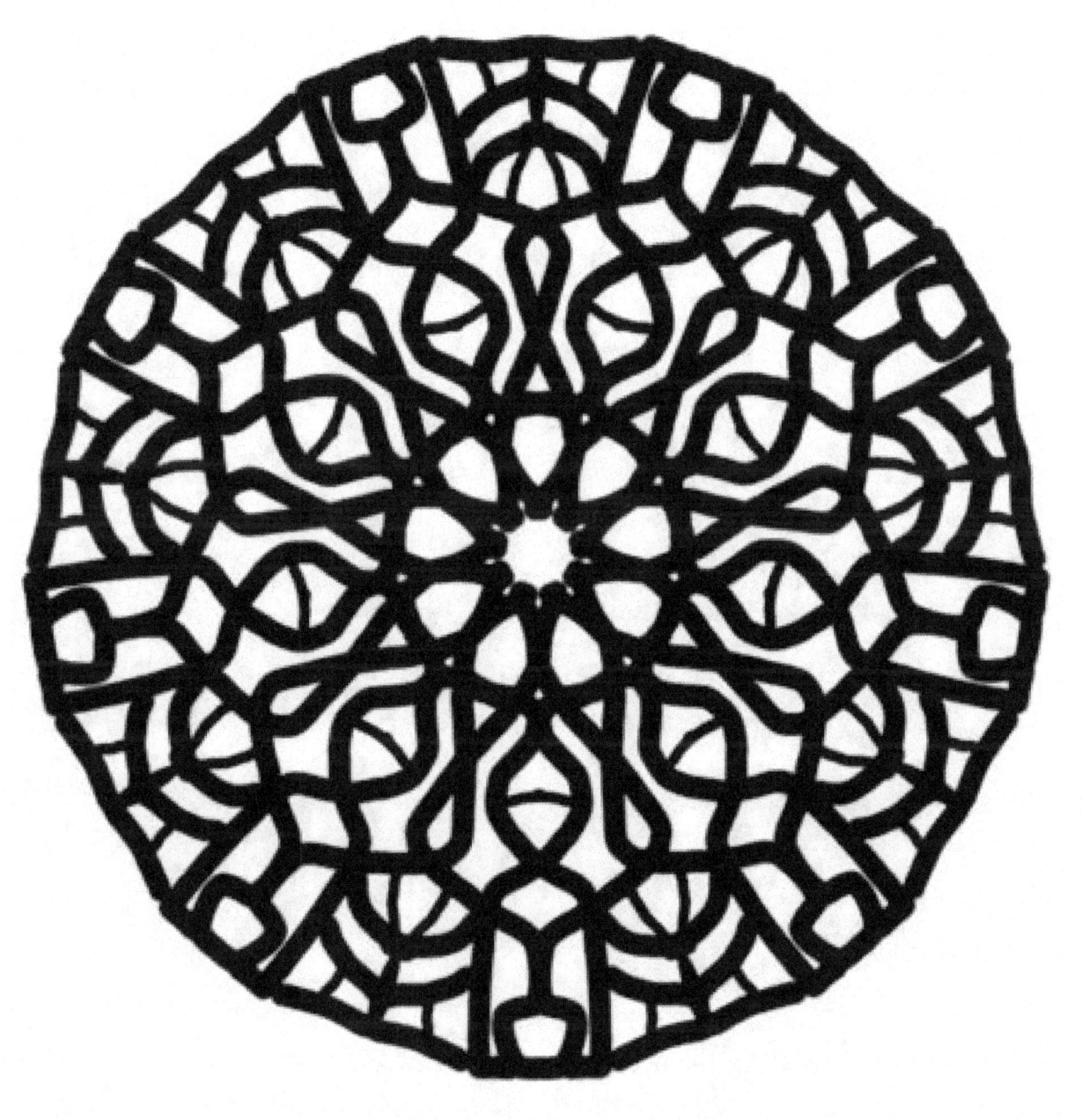

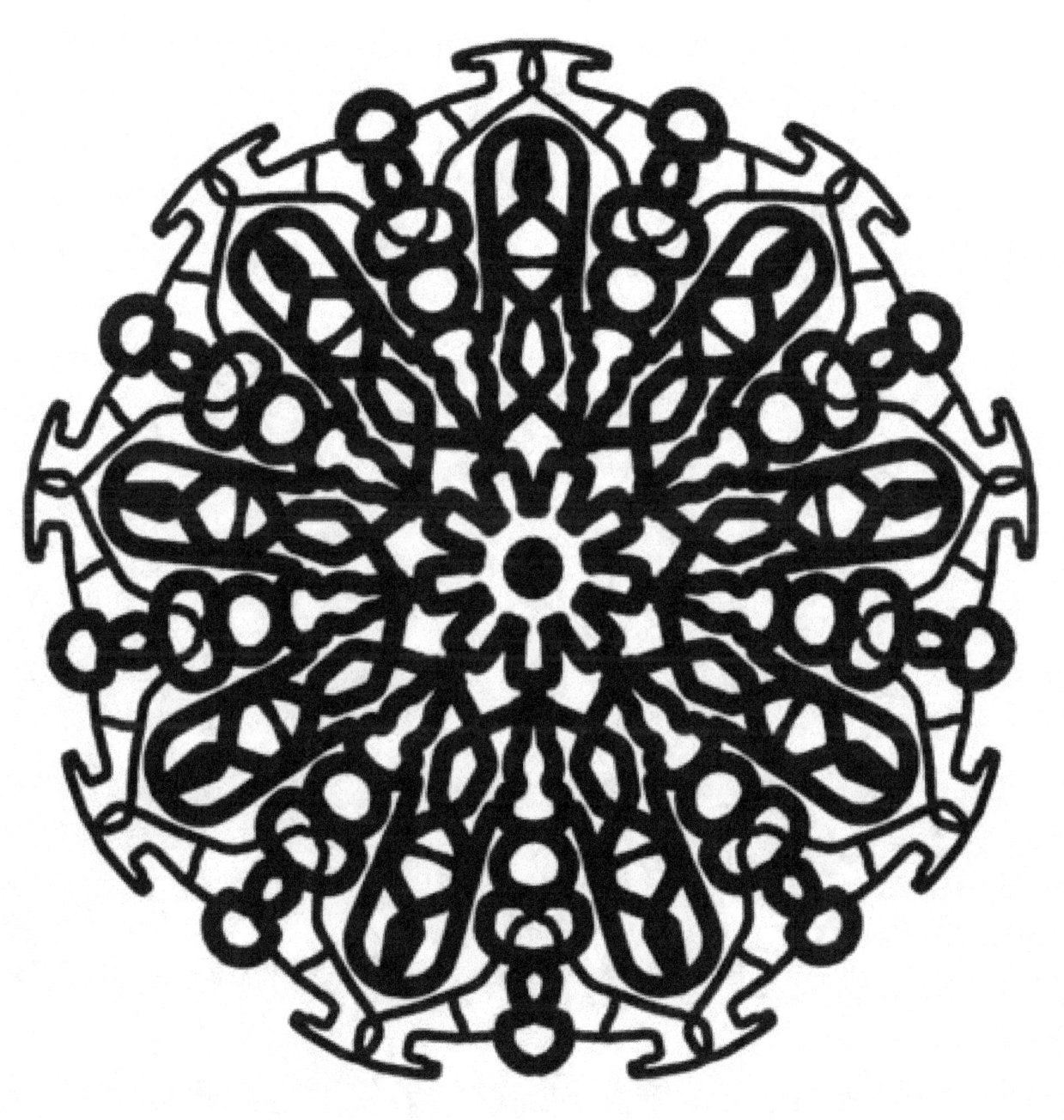

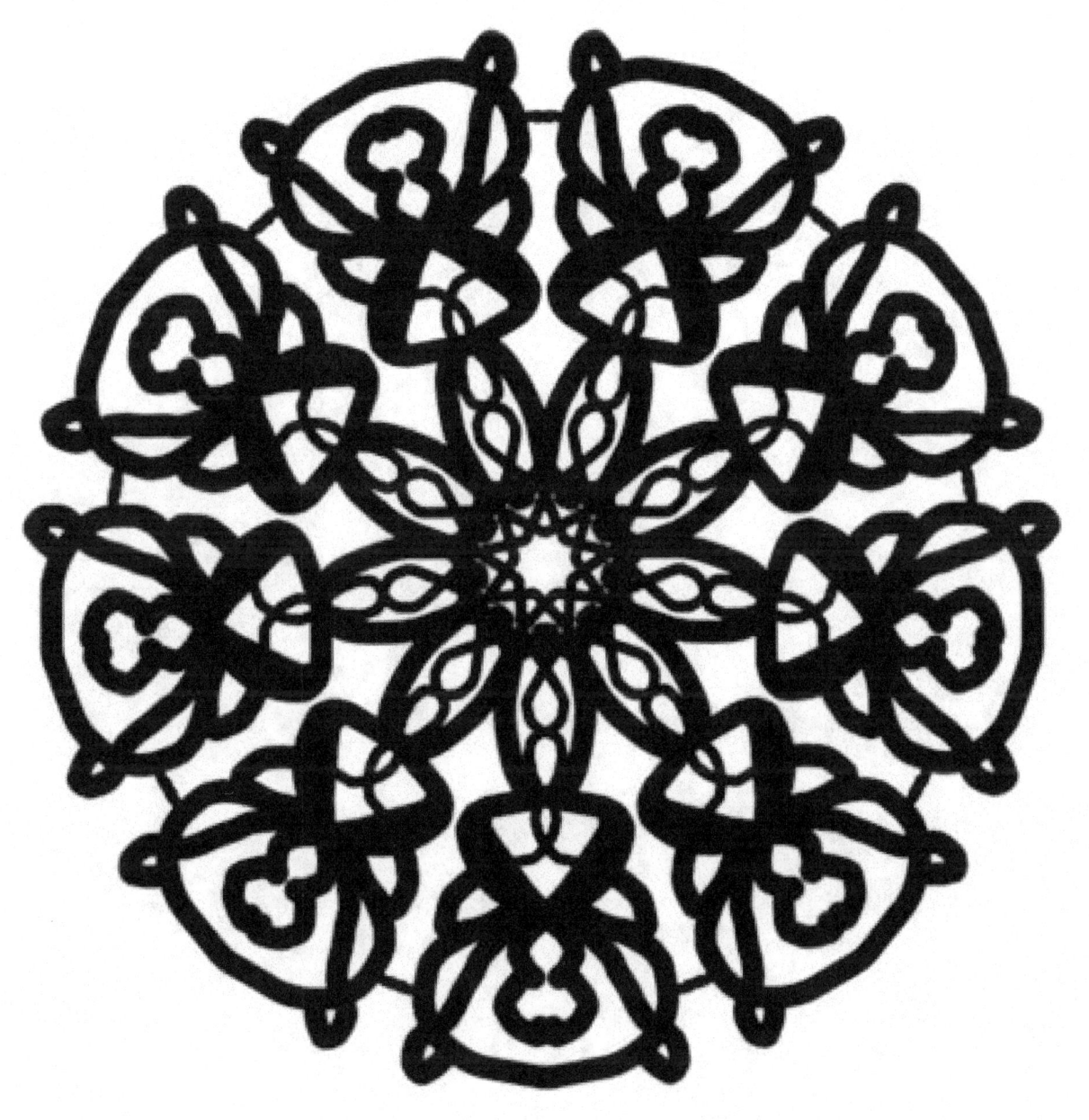

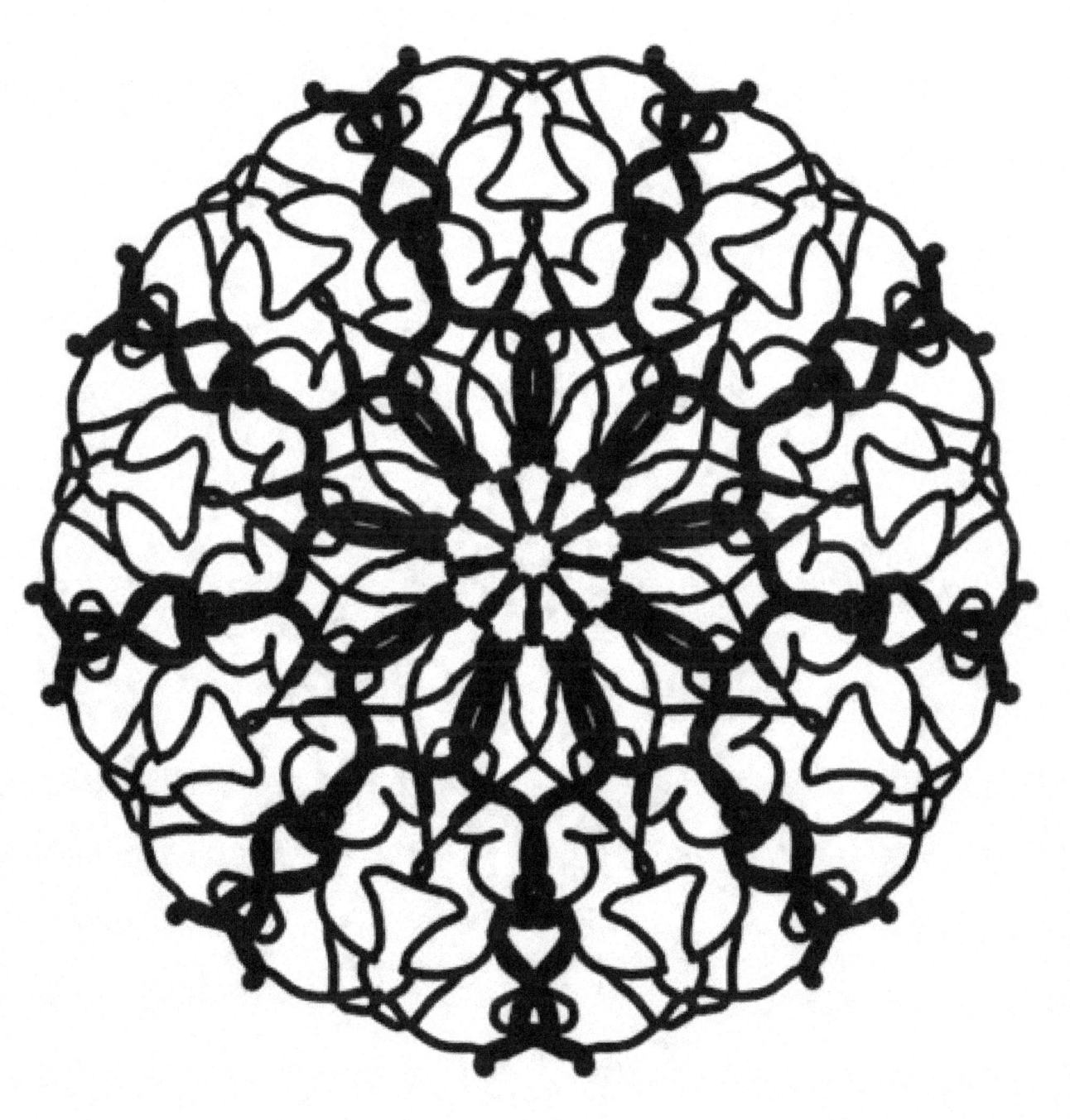

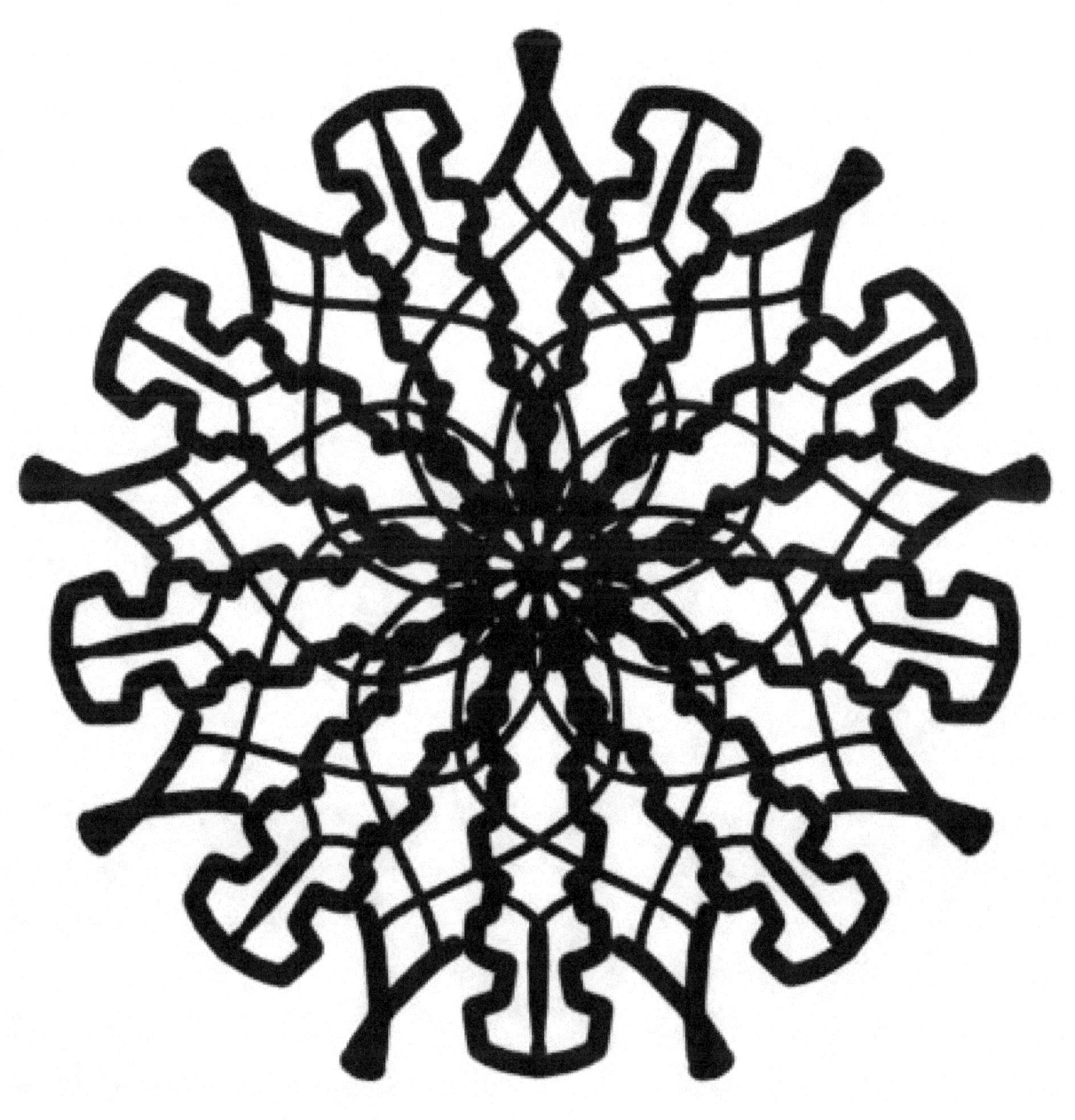

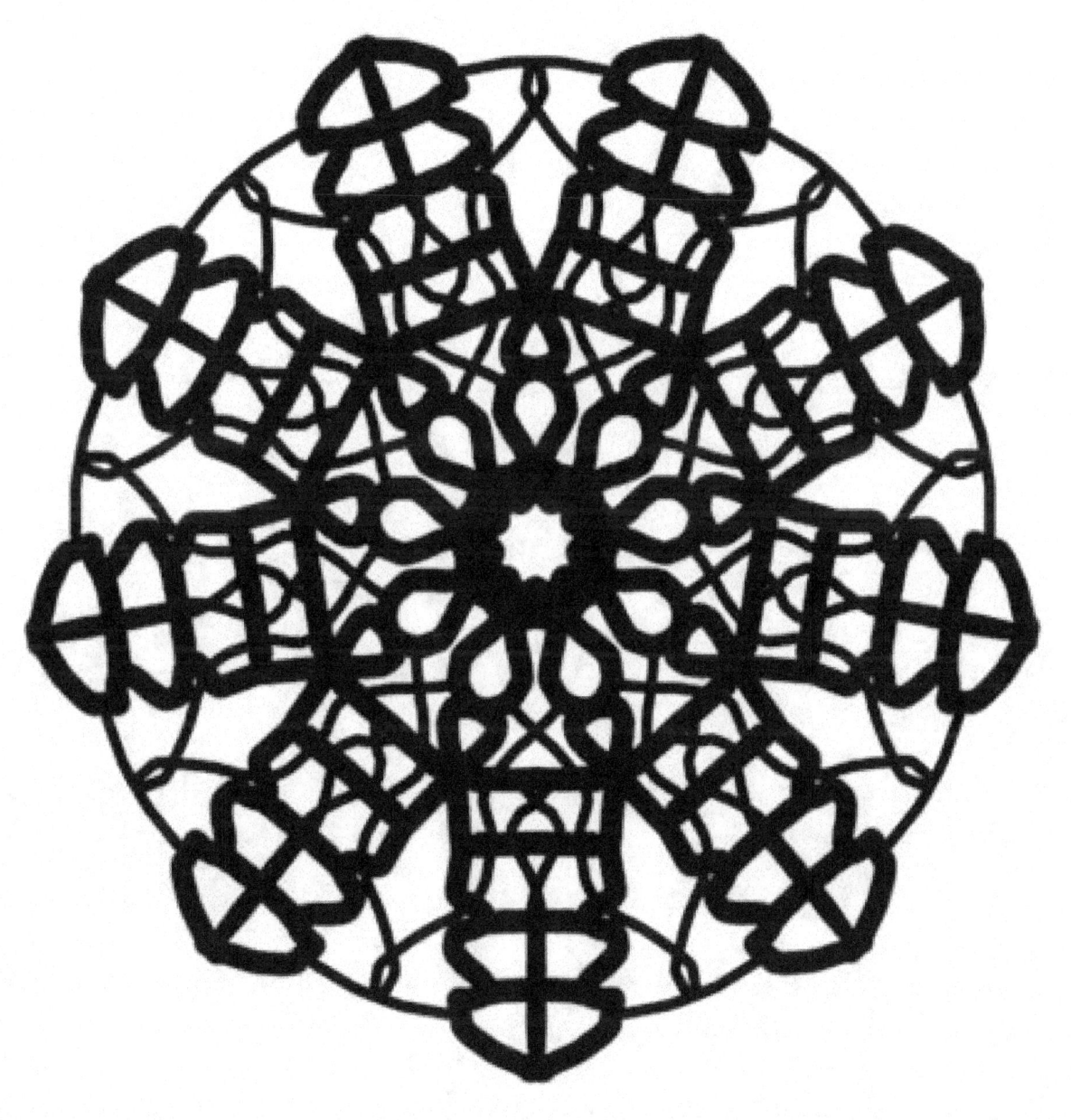

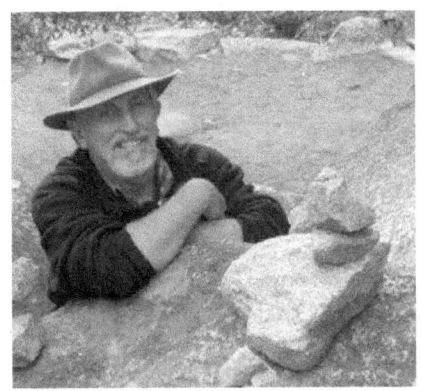

Ray Tucker

Ray's Creations
Studio / Gallery / Workshops
5178 Valley Center
Covina, CA 91723
(626) 705-6241

www.ingramcontent.com/pod-product-compliance
Lightning Source LLC
Chambersburg PA
CBHW081311180526
45170CB00007B/2653